INSECTS

INSECTS

Poems by
Iain Deans

Fitzhenry & Whiteside

Fitzhenry and Whiteside Limited
195 Allstate Parkway
Markham, Ontario L3R 4T8

In the United States:
121 Harvard Avenue, Suite 2
Allston, Massachusetts 02134

www.fitzhenry.ca godwit@fitzhenry.ca

Fitzhenry & Whiteside acknowledges with thanks the Canada Council for the
Arts, the Government of Canada through its Book Publishing Industry
Development Program, and the Ontario Arts Council for their support of our
publishing program.

10 9 8 7 6 5 4 3 2 1

National Library of Canada Cataloguing-in-Publication

Deans, Iain, 1973-
     Insects / Iain Deans.
Poems.
ISBN 1-55041-856-4
     I. Title.
PS8607.E25I58 2004   C811'.6
C2004-900391-7

Publisher Cataloguing-in-Publication Data (U.S)

Deans, Iain, 1973-
     Insects / Iain Deans.–1st ed.
[96] p. : photos. ; cm.
ISBN 1-55041-856-4 (pbk.)
1. Canadian poetry – 21st century. I. Title.
811.54 dc22   PR9195.72.D436 2004

Cover/text design: Karen Petherick, Intuitive Design International Ltd.

Cover art: Jennifer Harrison, Detail from *Small Patch of Snow Left at the Bottom
of the Hill*, 2003, Oil on canvas

Printed and bound in Canada

For Jennifer Gresham

CONTENTS

PART ONE

Insects

I am making you a ring in the form of a mathematical equation. I have been scratching out the numbers and symbols with India ink. My movements across the page have been like the short thrusts and stabs of an insect.

The formula is based on the solution to Fermat's Theorem. That solution required the invention of entirely new systems of mathematics.

Like our union, it can only exist on a highly abstract plane. Like the ballet of angry horseflies. Like the art of thousand-year-old millipedes pulling an army of appendages across the sand. Or the percussive music of cockroach feet on linoleum floors.

The formula is partially hinged on the existence of imaginary numbers. Like i. Lowercase, and forever trapped by cummings. Like me. Imaginary numbers for a lover I am bound to on paper. Letters, back and forth. In this letter a formula. A proposal in abstract. In yours a reply.

And so on.

If you answer yes, I will trace the formula on your right breast with an ant leg dipped in ink.

When we make love, we will be transported into the realm of applied theory.

And insects.

Something Was Growing Us Out There

Something was growing us out there
in fields thickened by bricks and trademarks
the wild spaces near the edges of empty parking lots
where shoes mumble against asphalt and
stolen cigarettes are tickled into life over
beer and boxes of wine
Dead Kennedys Black Flag and jeans from The Gap
we were conmen measuring our conversations
outside hollow malls late at night
our condoms twitching in the back of K-cars
where curfews shrugged and let themselves out
whispered confessions when our parents
left us alone in finished basements
so angry we had to take our clothes off
to fall in love
and always a voice on the periphery
issuing a warning we could not hear
the streetlights burned
like lipstick grins
while our melancholy poses slept
and our fathers
ran for their lives

The Bottom Of The Night

You laugh and call me a gambler
a rumour of water
polluting your drink

The music is slow
drowning in jokes
weighed like pieces of meat

And God I love this getting lost
the smell of peppermint on a stranger's breath
the rare impression made by a conversation

that slips through all the traps
a carpet eager to drink every mistake
while broken glasses project a dark sink

into a splash across the ceiling
the unnatural constellation speaking
to a friend lying on his side

the tiles cool against his face
as he searches for his place
in this reckless descent

For You, Three Occasions, In Dirt

1. Digging

I am digging a hole in the backyard. My shovel scalps the topsoil, each thrust makes the earth wheeze. I am going down deep, deep enough that each cloud of dirt can barely find the sky. Each cloud lies naked, waiting.

I lie down. I close my eyes against the blue window. I ignore the smeared clouds. The burning eye of the sun. I want to lie with worms. Feel cold earth snuggle against my back, wet the creases of my jeans, press its palm against my hair. Listen to the dull hum of sound overhead. Each breath loading my nostrils with a recipe of loam, clay, pebbles.

And I will think of you. In this, my first dirt mansion. A hiding place for you to find me.

I will rise at night when the sky and dirt are one. When I can pass from the edge of my home into your arms seamlessly, without the friction of colour.

I will let you wash me with sponges you have wet with your tongue. Each stroke of the sponge against my skin another step forward in time, another step away from the history of sand, the clock of soil.

2. Tunneling

Gone again. I will turn our room into a lair. I need mud. Thick and red from the Bay of Fundy, brown Mississippi, Amazon, ancient Nile. Swamp flesh pregnant with life. Dust from sidewalks, stones cast out like rebels from sandboxes.

I will paint our room a thousand shades of brown. Imagine the air thick with sweat, dampness a million years old. Warm. A womb. Fissures making maps as mud turns sand turns stone. Everything breathing beach dust.

My body covered, muscles cracking mud. Skin pulled tight. Fingernails buried forever.

I will greet you when you come back. I will emerge out of the earth, tribal, a man you only know by smell. Only in beaches, deserts. I was the ancient one feeding the bog. I was the one in the cliff wall, giving a piece of myself to the tide.

I will leave myself all over you.

I will dry your lips with my age.

3. Burying

I take the photographs out of the stained albums.

In the desert the sand is the colour and temperature of an oven element turned on high. A scattering of pictures. You, wrapped in nothing but green satin and shadow. You, drunk on vodka, eyes somersaulting. You, exposing your skin, your breasts embarrassed. All falling under grains of sand that tic-tack their way across each image.

Waiting for time to swallow you. For you to become treasure. Something to be discovered when the desert's slow ocean delivers you back to the shore of its constant beach.

I wash the dust from my feet. Each grain has traced your face as gently as the tip of a fingernail. Each grain knows you better than I do.

Thirty Years

The bathtub cups my shins
tap weighing down my hair until I am
swallowed by static, until I am 21 again,

running off a dock, summertime against my skin
Lake Rosseau at 1 am, a darkness so complete
the moon shatters across its surface rudely

broken by Acid gymnastics, and of course
I panic, tearing the black in half, water
rushing eyes, ears, the world a numb elbow

and I punch through, gasping, ready to inhale
a star and instead catch my heart between
my teeth, the chemicals playing my mind

like some rare Chinese instrument, hands
grasping my slick arms, pulling me out
of the water and into laughter, the sky

punctured with white light and a woman's blonde
hair invading my mouth as I try to kiss her, her
fingers pointing to No and candy on her breath

but I know exactly how my hands fit against her
hips – the drugs change direction and out I go
between the trees, whispering promises

that I plan to keep, and deep in the night's oil
I slide through the bushes thirsty, searching
for beer or answers and come back with nothing

but a thick tongue, hands accented with dirt
and splinters, smiling, eyes broken open into
perfect red gems kaleidescoping over trees

that fold in on themselves and explode

When the sun stretches its arms across the lake
I come down, slowly, a man stepping
off a train and into a strange city, and fall

into a long forgotten sleeping bag farming dust
in the last hours before we leave
I lean back – my new belly is an island

and the bathroom is smooth and clean
I eat bread every morning and
I don't remember my dreams

A Difficult Commute

In November everything dies beautifully
like a dancer in a rented room
Now Toronto can confuse us by shining at night
after days spent in alcoholic gloom
There is nothing grayer than Warden Ave. at 3 pm
the clouds hanging low
the hangman wiping his nose in a suburban Tim Hortons
I am the right kind of coward: I stretch
my tripwires at night and march to work
every morning
My quarrel is simple and therefore contagious
I will share it with you over lettuce and cough drops
my constitution owes back taxes to the government
Please understand I have no choice in the matter
I kill strangers in elevators every chance I get
pulling the trigger inside my head while making
vague excuses about my wardrobe
I am beautiful in my tan pants
I have written memos about everything

Adultery

This cold fish hook
a tug at the guts

but first wrapped
in sun

flat on the sheets
I should have

seen through you
and now

and now the carpet
wears down

the soles
of my feet

Noah On The 17th Day

So Noah
600 years old
and sick of it all
is standing on his boat
his Pandemonium
three-storeys high
and quite literally
full of life
finally tired
of the way
his wife
catalogues
their neighbours
as they bob by
wearing a coat of ha!
to warm her body
tired of going
below decks
threatening
sheep monkeys
moose
with marinades
and the grill
just so he can
sleep
his sons
more like
hyenas
every day

tearing into
each other
over endless
games of
poker
tired of the madness
in the clouds
drunk on
galaxies
the rain
applauding
against the
roof
so he lowers
himself down
into a lifeboat
nodding on the
gray on gray
cratered by rain
soaked to the skin
floating away
and
of course
they all call out to him
growls and screams
and whistles and words
but they can't have him

this morning Noah
is deaf
and grinning
he slices
the water
with his line
and waits
quietly
to kill a
fish that
is fat
white
and full of
cruel victories

The Silverfish

The silverfish are armoured   prehistoric
they move   in sentences
all stops and
starts
the bathtub is wet   streaked photography
of geographical extremes
time lapse evolution   of imaginary
continents   reservoirs caught
in the ivory cup
          of a cool hand

Tuesday
pauses to dry its
face against the curtains' black wrinkles
petrified mid slither

          This morning
was the morning
everything was unearthed

          and named again

Flak

I was lectured by your movements
Even your sulking felt like ambition

I'd come home
and your stare
would dim the lights

So
you left

and you left a
note with instructions for
a kind of life

You know
last night the
radio
played a hundred love songs

not one was about
someone like you

The Conversation

For weeks he carried the conversation in his wallet
his credit cards became loathsome
oiling the air with the scent of shit
his money rebelled and rented out muscle
to anyone who called and knew the right names
he was on speaking terms with no one but
the conversation
                              It woke him every night
to present him with the gift of argument
drilling its accusations deep into his skull
where they prospered
                                        calculating doubt
like a butcher in front of that final door

It is easy to be careless about these things
they have names and cannot be controlled
their eyes open like secret notes
the density of what they have to say
is heavy
and worthless at any market
but still deadly in the company
of the noose
the light switch
the drunk spies
force marching time
while he fumbles his manners
and gives in to everything
they have to offer

Red Boxes

They mark our oldest grudge

A shrine by the highway
small red boxes overturned
exposing interiors the colour
of burnt coffee grounds
the candles extinguished
thin bone fingers now
pointing at the road
directing me down a path
littered with animals
turned inside out
by drivers
who assemble
small altars
that smother
silently
on a gray
highway
that gathers its victims
with a patience
that is boundless
and unforgiving

"His interpretation was beautiful."

The commanding officer played on, even when the walls
trembled from bombardments and soil trickled down.

We can imagine the soldier telling the story later
his hands   shuddering like stars
The commanding officer had his bunker constructed
      beneath the snow
a chamber large enough for Mozart
Bach
his long fingers   white within the gloom
          cool and slow
finding the notes like a man
    caressing a lover
The dust hovering overhead
clinging to the steam
     retreating
into the darkness   with every pink breath
the keys providing their own light
while an applause of steel blooms
through the bodies
of men wrapped in rags
      who piss on their hands
their fingers black
against the frozen white that
swallows their thick red chorus
silently

They Were Beating Pig Boy

They were beating Pig Boy on the third base line:
one boy rode Pig like a horse   the others
lined up to take one two three quick steps
and
          then a kick releasing a belly howl that
painted Pig red and filled his lungs with reeds while
          the boys with voices
that can be heard everywhere
                                        bruised the sky
                                        and tore the gravel
with their feet

I watched   from the outfield
trapped by evergreens   and my own awe
too bright shoes swallowed by grass   dry eyed
as they reloaded
                    quietly dreaming   of membership
in this tribe
so willing to ride

one of its own
into the ground

Cool Surgical Hands

A liquid expectation slides between the gears
seducing mental vertebrae and paralyzing the mind

:he reveals himself for just a second through
a graininess found in movies featuring
the abuse of flesh   a description of
trembling hands above oil spill pants

Left alone, the body reaches a state of creeping flow
questions are ambidextrous; miraculous card tricks
are unleashed

There are no streets left

no places to go where the telephone throats
have been slit by cool surgical hands

We will bet our future
on a mechanical monster
who is good with words

The Woman In Wenceslas Square

You slumber
painted onto your chair
bent over
a coffee mug tilted
beneath one of your breasts
lips split
for a single breath

I want to touch your hair the
colour of wood chips
picture it fading into ash
blurring against skin
turned into crushed leaves
under the sun
shattered against the clouds
each one waiting
alone

Elegy For An Empty Film Set

It is nowhere now
        shrouds and dead angles
                naked without
                        calculation

the buildings are as they were
        forgotten above the door
                the predictable cars

chase no one
the spotlights remember nothing   blind behind
loose wires and armour

everything is gray Sunday again

                and
        Hollywood far away and
in a language
        without weather

           and you just stand there
as your street gathers its clothes

                and turns away

Côte des Neiges

The saltwater sheets hold July
against you like a tongue
You are not a monk whose desperation
can be swallowed by robes,
the phone does not ring,
there will be no confession.
Standard Life's imperial eye stares out
from among black and blue buildings,
tears the clothes off the night, follows
every stiff-backed last minute obsession,
every drunk who finds himself on
St. Catherine street screaming into the faces
of strangers, Americans, the lost.
You lock your windows and peer through the blinds
sure that outside the grinning
all-night monsters are meeting in garages and
alleyways, calculating the cost
of selling you to their howling master,
the raw spaces in his mind.

Montreal

You have no answers for me,
it's Sunday night, every
night you celebrate something I don't understand
I walk in my white socks and admire your leather
this city has flare – pay no attention to me
you never pay attention to me, my ten dollar hair
your women dressed black as streets

In February, St. Laurent carried me like a
stretcher when the ice swept my feet, when
I was covered in beer
I got an applause from passing cars as my breath
mushroomed out of me, and I wanted to stay there
and count the passing words, the ones I could
comprehend
      winter would have held me until morning,
      winter is always ready to give a hand to a man who
has forgotten his options

It's September now,
I'm drinking alone – if you don't count Cary Grant –
he's trying on suits on TV
I'm drinking beer and writing to you
I have an excellent job, sometimes
I take codeine pills to help me sleep
I don't blame you; I came this way
please forgive me
it's late at night, the weekend is setting,
I have no one else to talk to

After She Dismissed The European Masters For Being Slaves

It was as though the paintings never existed
no painter created them   no canvas felt a caress
and then held it for centuries
she dismissed an entire faith
like the plot to a particularly bad movie and
walked through the gallery like a queen
          no lightning from above
the moment let her pass

the moment let her pass
and there were no questions

On Signal Hill

It had been a
violent coronation
a crown of broken glass atop
the ashes of a stolen fence
a plastic bottle of rum
flanked by rocks ready
to address the cigarette butts
the brown paper bag
a forgotten blue jacket
tossed onto the grass
and tortured
by the wind

Up here the ceremony
would have been
largely ignored
a small fire on the
edge of the world
a momentary
king born of alcohol
and shattered glass
a minor priest baring
his skin to an indifferent
sea
slick eyes beneath
the surface
uninterested in a
flickering star
suddenly obscured
by the last dancer
her hair traced

by embers riding
the final sigh
of burning royalty

I am part of this now
watching the harbour
wait
ready itself
for the fall of day
its arms spread wide
for the dark shapes
that lurk on the edge
of another evening
plotting kingdoms
and the many ways
they are overthrown

The Gifts That Poison Us

The rabbit's guts corrupted until it erupts foam
and ragged seeds
the scar just below her bottom lip where
the car door found her on her knees
already in tears
every sidewalk crack he had to cross
her legs spread like an invitation
the dog that faded out of her arms   the
notes they both kept   where
everyone is accused of being an executioner
all the tactics of guerilla warfare
                    hit and run   evasion picking so
that they never scar   but remain bright
wet   impossible to ignore
all wrapped in the most expensive paper
waiting to be opened by experienced technicians
with sweaty fingers

Warden Ave.

The bus lurches down Warden Avenue
like a drunk searching for spare change

inside it's hot and wet as a throat
our bodies falling into every stop

drowning in August
carrying faces worn down

by hours inside a box
the windows lie to us

because we have made a bargain

we will not see that laughing woman
hair hanging in front of her eyes

like fingers crossed
to break a promise

The Painter

A delicate pain,
the longing of mud; ash spread
on canvasses cracked as ancient skin
a room full of typewriter exoskeletons
landscapes rejected for hands, twisted
wire and jagged tin
bitter charcoal faces and smoke
that reaches and fails and reaches
– waits for me with chemicals corroding
her palms
peels open her stories like a
car crushed on an expressway

Rue Ste. Catherine

In a way
water brings out
the best in you
streetlights
admire themselves
in puddles painted
with gasoline
your crown of graffiti
stands out   red and
yellow dragons
furious clouds
above wet

skeleton trees
lonely savage in
an old man's jacket
all evening I staggered
across your carpet
of reckless leaves
as your cars crawled like
beetles
                    and smelled like
blood

The Condition

The avalanche pauses at your door, and smiles.
Of course the radio is on, the television too.
Everyone has a plan, a dedication they have written.
The tub is overflowing in the bathroom.
Your wardrobe starves in the birdcage.
The relatives are rioting over dinner.
A toy soldier is tortured in the living room.
The dog begs for fingers.
I am upside down in the snow.
My toes are very brittle.
The doorbell is on fire.
Nobody knows how guilty you are.

Lorenz's Clouds

A sensitive dependence on initial conditions
something unaccounted for   ignored
can create vast change,

a physics   numbers that move

a butterfly being alive   stirring the air today in Tokyo
can transform storm systems
next month in New York

Imagination: a daydream has a theory

                          a box of monarchs
orange and black   brittle,
static cardboard

opens: and the colours smoke out
                          into the sky

an eclipse and motion
a box in my hands   waiting
                     for a change in the clouds

for the things that are to be

This Spider Like A Hand

This spider like a hand with fingers spread
a palm searching

this web a place a vision spun in song
in thin string   Spreading across branches
of flexible physics,

a growing place   a space between thoughts.

This hand
with fingers spread waves itself across
growth and status

            This is the spider this hand
this constant hello of fingers
this fascination with balance

              and threads like thought.

From The Mantelpiece A Message

The stone Buddha you gave me gets up,
lotus freed knees shaking off dust and

now ready to float, but instead a pause
to breathe in the wow of it all and

I'm frozen in my chair when
he says your name beach sand smooth

reaches me on powdery feet, rough fingers
clink against teacups, expresses

an interest in the exchange of notes so that
we may better paint the you who

passed through us both when you thought I
needed a guardian, and he needed a home

you should know that we are both
satisfied with the arrangement

we have signals to send you
look for our faces everywhere

A Whisper In The Matchbox

Our impulses
and the gravity
of our situation
work against each
other the way a border
splits a war: I
wish I had
the patience to
make the investment
to take the time to find you
flowing like a glass
a shadow in deep space
waiting to be exposed
and therefore erased
a blink of light
bending time
with its
decisiveness
exploding everything
with its motion
a whisper in the matchbox
I threaten
immolation
when I need you

They Won't Find Us

The crowds rub their eyes against
the windows.
But they won't find us. Not up here
catching lips, the day holding
its breath until the walls turn blue

Let them shred their ambition on
the blades of steel buildings:
I reject the howling meat that
fills my courtyard with
excessive vowels

Forget the traffic packed like bullets,
nothing but waves against the shore
The hungry shoes that have taken
the avenues can have them

Let them have it all
I won't stutter

You tear a hole in their insistence when
you spill your clothes in the hall
They are gravel in a child's bucket
and we
we are cool reptiles
hiding from the sun

Glossolalia

Casual at first
the way cool drops of water
play a sink

but now curled against
my body
tight as a conch shell

my whiskers
brush your
back

and I am
full of
intentions

my lips know you
like a whisper

and then you
are awake

your body
bright and aware

find me beneath
the sheets

and show me
all your stories

I will read you
like a blind
man

when I am
with you

I want
to speak
in tongues

You're Such A Confessor, She Said

Soon I will have nothing left to carry.
The burden of my stories will
be shouldered by victims,
and I will have time to
write again.

PART TWO

The Clown Remembers

We were talking about a place to stay when you covered your eyes and stepped off the plane. I watched you fall for hours, your body spread out like wrapping paper, a fresh cigarette punctuating your teeth. When you tried to smile, I melted, and I remembered how it felt to stand on stage, lights swallowing my gaze, braids of milk running down my cheeks. I was a different man then – I wore a red nose and carried my cap in my hands. I never dreamed you would fall forever.

Statistics Show

That I don't know you.

I don't know how to compile this history.
Our language is measured in seismic rumbles.

Satellite photos are blurry, inconclusive. This is the
Mexico City of indecision. The sky is the colour of
dishwater. The windows are closed.

I refuse to hide my life like a reef breeding bitter poison.

Arthur Rimbaud can keep his sideshow. His African
desert is cold, and lonely at night.

Our moon is angry and full of answers.

I am stepping onto the wet edge of the world. I clutch
my umbrella. I smile.

Only the stars have sharper teeth.

Swimming

A man a floor
      he presses his foot to the floor
and falls into the ocean

This finger   this dream I had
I am tracing it for you

In the dark   my saltwater mouth
drips images

my feet leave little lagoons
on the approach   to your bed

my finger dancing in the air
sketching the things that happened

when I was blue
singing a song in bubbles

after I fell through the floor
having been thirsty   beside you

The Way The Dream Works

The lost space between wind and silence
suspends my attention the way
                                       an icicle
fights gravity

My face presses against the highway's
scaly skin
nose filled with mattresses
mouth with copper wire

There are headlights in the distance

Suddenly lizarding down the street
curtaining my face   blown back
from the Metro by a rubber wind   recoil
and the voices want to swallow you:

He's whispering   a gentle hiss above
the clicks of his work
                            the hunched muscle
crouches above his puddle of shadow
sorts bones in a government cavern

Come closer

There is always something to show you

and the wet subterranean urges
pulse against skin washed white by the rain

                         The car passes from blurry
to purring machine   pulls up to my knees

the door opens
the moon bellows

Ghost Box

Like a ghost's whisper
gliding down a wire
a voice in the morning
recorded metallic
in a dusty plastic box
push a button
and you are there
undecipherable even though
the English is perfect
a signature goodbye
and then gone
a door swishes shut
in the attic behind
my eyes
I can't make sense
of what you said
I am blind to messages
thrown through the air
carved in sand from
a distance
they wait in the kitchen
to ambush
over coffee
with the sun in my eyes
and my hair rebellious
listen:

Dotted Line

When I finally lay
upon you
with my frog belly
(too white)
I was content
without tattoos
In that room
filled with spider clothes
lines and
Japanese walls
our bodies
were efficient enough
without the arrogance
of signatures

Using My Days As Matches

I use my days as matches
playing the parrot in some stranded
sailor's tropical dream
No opinions any more, the elevator
sighs and drops us off at the office
a feline moon surrounds us
a careful index of atrocity
the purr of an electrician
caught against the circuits
steam and burning
denim
the paintings we hung
in the staircase so sure
we would only glance
at them
the snicker in the marketplace
the carved wood I threw
in the stove
a symbol of forgetfulness
a murder of circling crows

He Became A Carnival When He Drank

He became a carnival when he drank
as if the bells and whistles were there
for one night only
and admission was free
He ran from table to table
talking about everything
smearing the stories
like paint on canvas
until the storm set in
as it always did and
he fell back into himself
and counted his money
hoping there was one more ride
the sweat overtaking him
the ticket
staining his hand
like a scar

The Blue Silence

It is calm beneath the available illusions –
the billboards that mark
the shore of changing seasons

In the blue silence before morning
everything is forgiven
the streets are finally perfect

the trees clasp their hands
the grass becomes a thick
green virus

showers of insect song
fall on paths marked
by wrappers and ancient gum

hydro lines tense between their towers
stretch towards invisible machinery
vibrating into the longest note

of a dead century

the clumsy thump of streetlight
mechanics
shifts order without an audience

the cars hold their breath
as they harvest the sweat
of another night's indifference

some nameless splash of a bird
interviews tomorrow
in the first language we ever shared

and no one knows the river
its hidden flow of conversation
deep and cold as a distant galaxy

the stores are caged and divided
the highways are naked
exposing their argument

in favour of escape

That Morning

Stumble across a spill-stained floor
across its shifting borders and
into the shower   glue-eyed and
hungover   a second only
up on one heel
tickling the handrail   the water in my
lungs and my lungs
in my mouth's perfect O

The world is whole   is suddenly
perfectly defined: an
illustration of the inside of an insect
biographies of sweaty tiles
interviews with the soap sliding
out of its tray
every object a freshmen student
begging to be classified and understood

In the hallway plastic bags wait
to be mapped   last week's laundry
is tense and alive
and I hold my breath   and they hold theirs
until I'm swearing at the
shampoo painting my eyes
I am glad to be blind
I am glad that last night
I threw all the photos away

Walking Along The Edge Of Spring

Ice hangs off the sides of buildings
like loose skin
I am walking along
the edge of spring, watching the snow come down,
each flake a man falling through a dream.
The newspapers threaten me,
trains stitch this city closed,
I could strangle
a guitar neck to death trying
to break this down,
I am out here on the edge of spring,
and my engine is cold.

For days now, I have watched faces
break like windows
On Spadina there was a sign:
It's After the End of the World,
four feet high and drying.
That was seven years ago. I don't know
what to tell you.
The radio says there are men
being stacked like cords of wood
their hands bound with wire
that only wants bone.
The wind
clears its throat in the trees
and I know in my gut
that there are no words
violent enough to settle our debts.
I want to be a part
of a very dangerous machine.

Radio Reports From New York Indicate

The voices in the courtyard are petals
falling to the ground
the television takes a breath, and empties
the bedroom
the sky is blue, impossibly blue,
like paint
it is Tuesday morning,
and the monster is waiting
radio reports from New York indicate
the *Iliad* is darker than we think.

On Fenwick

The ferry is blind is a
satellite locked in a milky orbit
extraterrestrial cotton ball sliding
through the low harbour moan
foggy kisses: forehead, nose, lips
wet jacket, ignored
                Clouds drunk clumsy blankets
slightly rusty above the lights
bleeding paint water   trying to be seen
                And what if we still believed –

                That towering apartment building
greedy monolith on Fenwick –
hundreds of windows   luminous as polished skulls
We would fear your mastery   your concrete doom
so beautiful in its relentless conquest of now
                would scrape thick
scripture on highways waiting for oily torches to
invade our communications
              begging forgiveness for
some blunt sacrificial atrocity   galactic amber eyes
blinking off one by one as
the night rubs its forehead
exhausted
            Because it is late, it is late and
the heaviness slows me down to embrace
my stare   our
microchips will be worn
on the arms of violent men who
worship stars.

The Bananas Are Melting Inside Their Skin

The bananas are melting inside their skin
the days pass for each of us, their
perfume toffee sweet as they soften
within their freckled coats.

They do not contemplate the beer bottles
and the velvet splashes of green life
growing inside them. They pay no attention
to the knives drowning in the sink.

The broken spines of forgotten books
do not draw a sliver of pity,
they are content among the scattered papers,
the desperate notes, the stains from Thursday's dinner.

They don't pay tribute to the lonely phone.
The way I whisper to the room, fingers
raking my hair, does not fill them with doubt for
even a second.

The Other Trouble

In the end
the apartments across the street
will be incendiary bellowings sucking the air
out of everything around them.
I'm not sure if I have checked out of
some rude foreign hotel
or if the roots of that kind of pretension
have finally found me
the difficulty of this moment
is complicated,
tribal madness passed on like
a baton from one crouching
hairy mute to another at
train stations, revolutions,
and sale-priced interrogations
live on TV.
It's the clumsiness that's appalling
                    And there I go
backwards into the hedges
intoxicated by my
delicate Braille hypocrisy.
Drunk happy vendor
we both know
my loans are long
long overdue.

I Am Told About A Dog

I am told about a dog
burnt black as oil
simmering flies
beside a Mexican road

the mind's shadow   demands
possibility
we grasp the gas can

with our incantations securing us
the encryption on the splinters
of the soul   securing us

until the lines have been crossed

and we stand inside our skin
                              our faces crowded
by the cloudy flames
willing to bet everything
                    on the cruel white
grin that

knows our darkest gods
the forgotten laws
                    of our bloodiest priests

Paul Verlaine

*After a dinner of stewed mushrooms and burnt
horsemeat, he punched his pregnant wife… On
a visit to his mother's house, he smashed the
pickling jars and sent his grisly siblings
swilling across the floor.*

The jars spray their inheritance from mantelpiece
to floor
          the liquid embrace releases four pink arms,
the small bodies curled into question marks now
impossibly large against the carpet, and perhaps
he finally learns to recoil, his face red
from the argument, absinthe oiling his breath:
             the gray eyes own him
are moonlight through the curtains; the
dull exhaust of this place speckled with glass shards
that can never be stars even in the spasm
of twisted candlelight
              and what could he say
even as the words roar out of him like vomit
or a vision, what could possibly be left to write
to his siblings, the pickled lungs, his mother's screams
scalding the night?

Shower Stall

The shower stall is a gangster
that participates in every crime

                off-key singing
                the scent of guilty genitals

it is an accomplice
washing the evidence

            down the drain
a wet caress   wiping away orphan hairs
and tears: all kinds

has made you stand at attention
made you bow your head

                and close your eyes

has heard a million confessions

forgives you for everything

Hear Me Mirror

Wrapped in a towel
and a t-shirt
washing my face
wanting needing
to be born
a skull soul
explosion
the great
closed wilderness
cut open
by a heavy razor
galactic perfect
and at just
the right moment
slice my wordy
fullness the endless
memory film
hear me mirror
show me the
prayer I
must create

Every Night He Finds Her

Like some foul engine made of coal and bones
he bellows through the walls venting
his twisted steam
                                  and now my kitchen
is full of fists   my ceiling is a broken
door and   their lives shatter
the windows like stones
I must become the darkest man at the circus
the one who devours glass fire sin
I want to send her all my weapons

Every night I beg her to destroy him
while I chew my courage like a sow

Off The Coast Of California

The ritual is always
the same

Bull seals are slaughtered
by the Great White sharks
that commute beneath them

page after page
they remain shapeless
until the last
moment
a final shadow
          torpedoing
to the surface
a jaw
extending
to fill the world

we watch
as the body erupts
and stains the water
in these stolen photographs
we witness
the craftsmanship
of perfect
desire

The Answering Machine
Finally Demands An Answer

Is the mad professor dead in his apparatus
you asked

No   but there are a thousand televisions
that only want to talk
                    there is a nest of scars
in the coffee pot
                We never reach
the streetlights   all the sidewalks
are cool and clean
        everyone signs their name
on the side of a bus

So enjoy the candy
we have provided

I am told
that we are all
very fond of you

Jerry Lee Lewis

The final note is played with gasoline
searing the skin off his fingers
releasing the lonely angel
wailing through smoke
the faces melting after the tears
fuck the sweat and what is needed
is finally revealed

They break their knuckles on the walls
and scream until their throats fold
because they have to
the beautiful nightmare realized
Christ and the Devil fast asleep
as he tears the scalp off the kingdom
and kills his way through the night

I summon all the highways
the skyscrapers this useless paper
give me the ceremony
give me the currency to buy that moment
to press my lips against the charred piano
to finally know the taste
of that ruthless kiss

The Copywriter

He punctures his smile with a cigarette that says
I am in control this is what I planned
I am my own medicine

But the sweat finds him.

It is 8 pm and
the pages are restless

For weeks the deadlines have marched past
and now a tumour bolts his shoulders
he jigsaws his nails his
fingers thick with reluctant grace
and a love of words that are everywhere
that are nowhere

The coffee pot spits   clicks and stains his breath brown

They have strategies here
that can shave the edge off a miracle
elevators burrow through the building
as he hides in the bathroom
dreaming of a million kinds of escape
swimming in the simple dread known to men
who pace on carpets making fists

Oh anything for a roaring exclamation of flame
some ancient god or comic book ghoul
what does it matter   as long as the monster is there

to burn the white walls grey

to boil the water cooler clean
teeth obsidian sharp and ready to incinerate
the agendas the notes the phonebooks

timesheets coil back in slow black waves
the air shudders and retreats

slamming doors like textbooks
the firestorm
bends his coworkers into thin pink scars

But morning will come
will show up every day and wait for him

holding his jacket in its hands
until he knows who owns who
and who will last the longest

He picks up his pen
and tries to be brief

Maybe It Was Murder

The computer monitor hits the fifth-floor window so
hard the rejection ripples out

dead lit by fluorescent lights, up and
off the window again inflicting a seizure

and again making the window spider web, the
wires snapping along behind like a lost chance

then through and out, causing an
unnoticed eclipse, hanging for just a

second before facing downwards, descending,
two sheets of paper acting as reluctant

wingmen, hovering as the monitor plunges
and coughs on impact, imploding, loose clouds

silence and a passing
Buick, then music from above

the glass raining down

like laughter

4:54 am

He stumbles into the phone booth
alien change rains down onto
the sidewalk
he tries to remember
if Pennies From Heaven is a song
or a movie
                          the red wine
has starved
his fragile archives

He attempts to make the call
imagines the wires
running beneath the ocean
forgets about satellites
dials the wrong number
three times
                          snaps his leash
crashes the receiver
against the key pad
until it bleeds
                          a foreign voice

He gets through
there is some mumbling
and repetition

In Budapest the sky is
purple   creased
                          he imagines her breasts
the way she rested
her chin on his sternum

He can't remember what he is talking
about

When the phone suddenly dies
he thinks about money

imagines pennies falling
from a velvet sky

High Tide

1

scratch holes in the ink until
there is a coastline

there is so much here
I can't name

you become a cipher
counting the passing moments that

roll across the curtains
in waves,

unclassifiable,

the island is half-complete,
chaotic

an absence of narrative about
the place, there

is a history, but even it pulses
randomness: pregnant ships

that erupt on the edge of reefs,
false beacons,

tides that never set their graveyards
free

sugarcane, rum, vans packed with reggae and
limbs

roofs that yawn at the
sun:

a place where the scenery dreams
and what is real

only changes

2

assemble a separate dictionary,
there are words that fall away

precise   order   time

a river of colours unwinding shadows,
under the spell of this lexicon

everything flows,
you will become

lost in so many ways,
the salt finds lips

and fingers grasp at nothing

develop this allowance for emptiness

the ocean will find your ears

there are thirsty mouths
full of answers

3

unlike the sharp feet of this
sand crab, you will not tell

your story to the sand

watch: the claws are pulled up
against the shell in

a prayer too old
and deep to understand, sink

to the thick blue place
where these things

are written in currents

:and still things come back

4

at night, the lights capture
the palm trees

sweat on the balcony
and remember:

a man fading into the lake
his finger pointing out his riddle

all night we carved the water for
an answer, by morning

our behaviour had become
vernacular,

looking back, this was a vision
you must understand how

these things happen

the liquid delirium,
the necessity of our fevers

5

you start to feel the phantom

the birds slip through
the blinds to steal our

bananas,

imagine them that night
sweet and victorious

this is not like us, the
husk of a gecko curled

into a c, dry and light
as silk

6

listen:

with quiet sentences
we will become

invisible to machinery

this is a promise

7

the moment you fall off
the page:

the sliver of expensive
china ejected from the sea

it slipped through somewhere,

one of history's
uncomfortable moments

among the shell fragments: it was
a kind of exit, the last

way out of all the
essays
its own mystery
unraveling you

we were so close
to it all then

8

unlike it all, if you can
excommunicate

at night they scour the shore
with lanterns,

smoking on the sand
you can say

whatever you need to be

confess: you are becoming
electric

even the breeze
will pull you apart,

and vibrating now

understand

9

unroll,

this is not our ocean
this is the pedigree of fiction

a memory half-believed,

becoming a daydream

on Crane Beach
this happens:

all the obscenity
of insect precision

evaporates

the tides can swallow
a man

swim with their sentences

the island was a sketch
for a reason

and now you must
become your fever

self: undone

Index of Titles

Part One

Acknowledgements

"Insects" first appeared in *The New Quarterly*.

"Insects", "From The Mantelpiece A Message", and "This Spider Like A Hand" were all featured in *New Canadian Poetry*, ed. Evan Jones (Fitzhenry & Whiteside, 2000).

"The Woman In Wenceslas Square" and "Ghost Box" both appeared in *Yield*.

"Dotted Line" appeared in *Prairie Fire*.

"For You, Three Occasions, In Dirt" appeared in *The Gaspereau Review*.

"Noah On The 17th Day" appeared in *This Magazine*.

The epigraph for "His interpretation was beautiful." was taken from Anthony Beevor's book *Stalingrad* (Penguin Books, 1999).

The epigraph for "Paul Verlaine" was taken from Graham Robb's *Rimbaud* (W.W. Norton & Company, 2000).

I would like to thank Shannon Babcock, Adam Pasquella, Chris Turner, Jodi Essery, Jenny Smith, Tyson Hynes and Melissa Marr for their support and input.

I would especially like to thank my editor, Evan Jones. His patience, insight and faith made all the difference.